POP PERFORMANCE PIECES

Trumpet & Piano

T0061459

Published by
Chester Music
part of The Music Sales Group
14-15 Berners Street,
London W1T 3LJ, UK.

Exclusive Distributors:
Music Sales Limited
Distribution Centre, Newmarket Road,
Bury St Edmunds, Suffolk IP33 3YB, UK.
Music Sales Pty Limited
Level 4, Lisgar House,
30-32 Carrington Street,
Sydney, NSW 2000 Australia.

Order No. CH85085
ISBN 978-1-78558-336-0

Piano scores are transposed.
Chord symbols at concert pitch.

Trumpet consultant: Toby Street.
Piano consultant: Lisa Cox.
Compiled and edited by Naomi Cook.
Music formatted by Sarah Lofthouse, SEL Music Art Ltd.

Photographs courtesy of Ruth Keating,
assisted by Lisa Cox and James Welland.
Special thanks to the pupils at St Benedict's School, Ealing
and their Director of Music Christopher Eastwood for taking
part in the photo shoot.

Printed in the EU.

Your Guarantee of Quality
As publishers, we strive to produce every book to the highest commercial standards. This book has been carefully designed to minimise awkward page turns and to make playing from it a real pleasure. Particular care has been given to specifying acid-free, neutral-sized paper made from pulps which have not been elemental chlorine bleached. This pulp is from farmed sustainable forests and was produced with special regard for the environment. Throughout, the printing and binding have been planned to ensure a sturdy, attractive publication which should give years of enjoyment.If your copy fails to meet our high standards, please inform us and we will gladly replace it.

www.musicsales.com

CHESTER MUSIC
part of The Music Sales Group
London / New York / Paris / Sydney / Copenhagen / Berlin / Madrid / Hong Kong / Tokyo

ALL OF ME

Words & Music by John Legend & Tobias Gad

Hints & Tips: Make sure you use the dynamics to help build interest in the piece, being careful not to overpower the melody. There are many held notes throughout — resist the urge to rely on the pedal to sustain the notes rather than holding them for their full value. Practise without the pedal first!

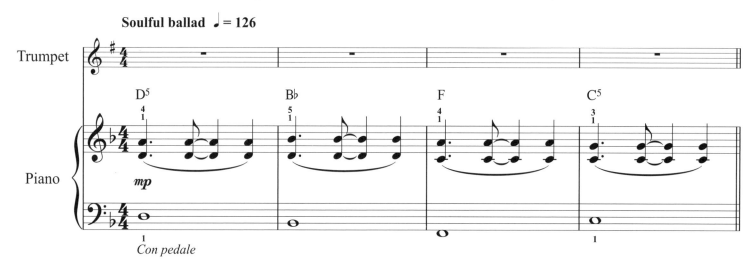

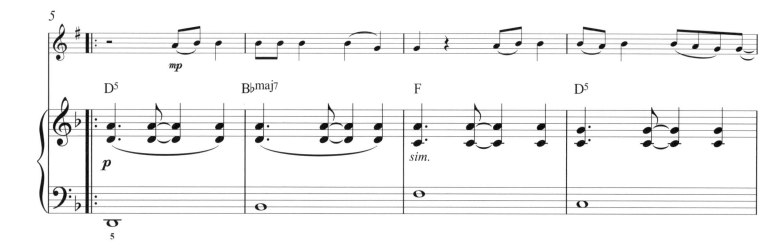

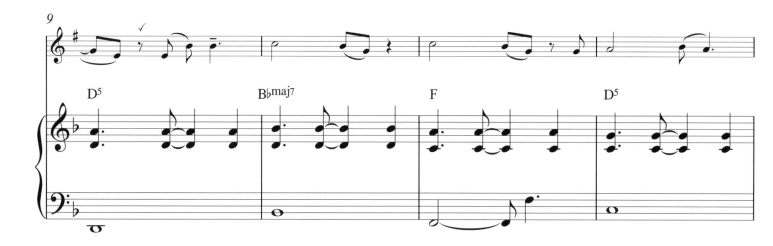

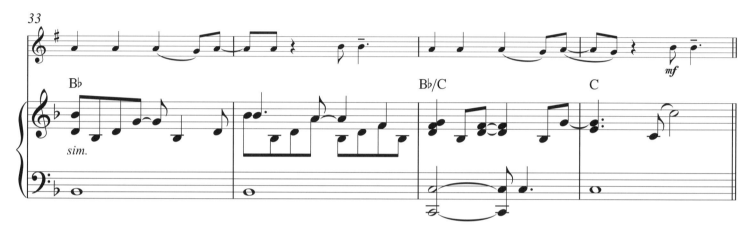

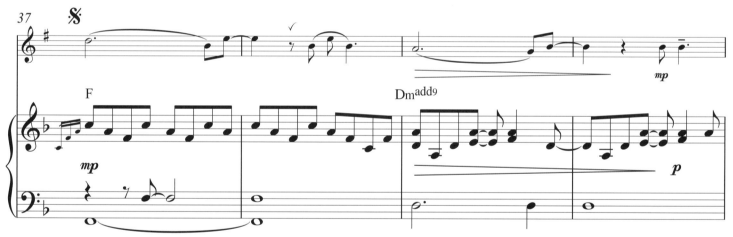

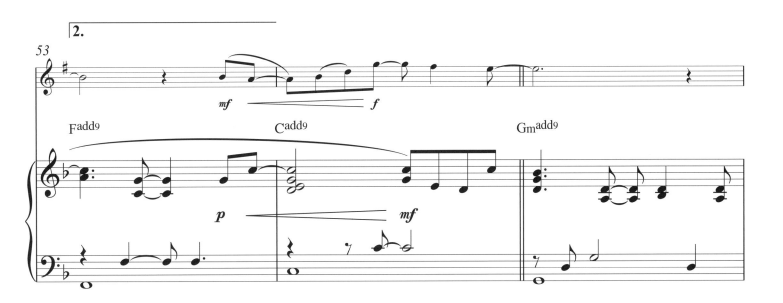

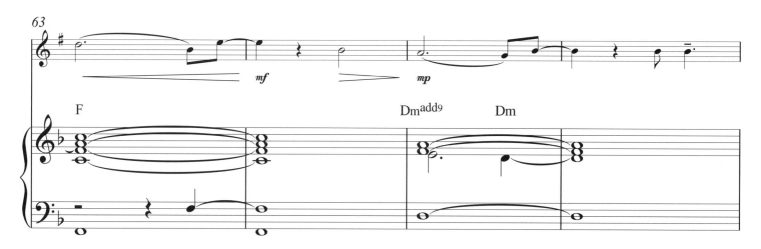

D.S. al Coda

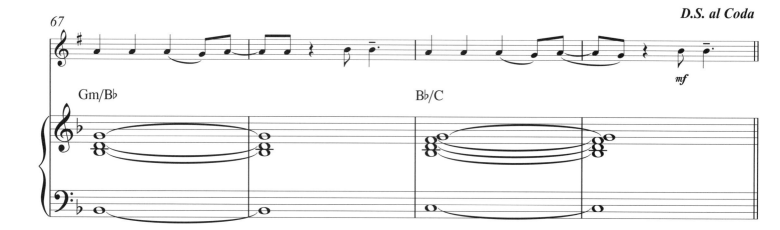

BRIDGE OVER TROUBLED WATER

Words & Music by Paul Simon

Hints & Tips: There are lots of block chords in this piece: make sure you use the correct fingers in anticipation of the next chord position. Watch out for the accidentals too!

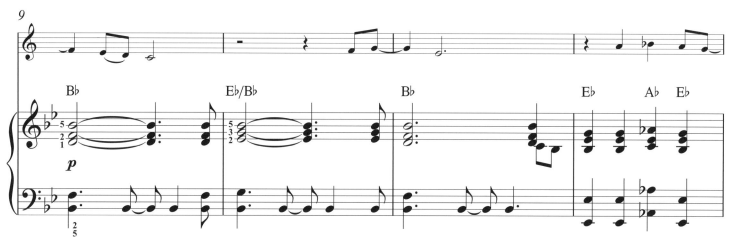

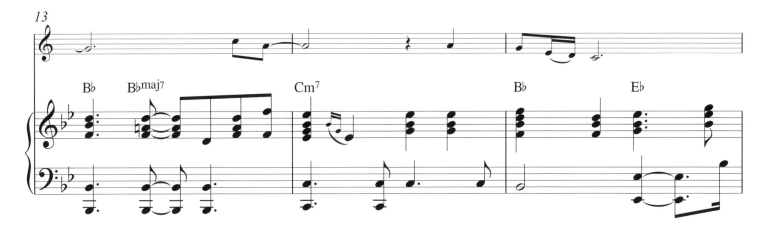

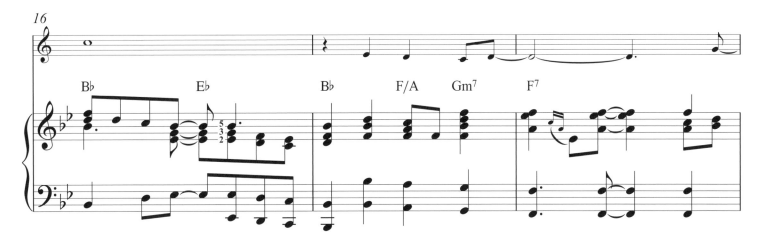

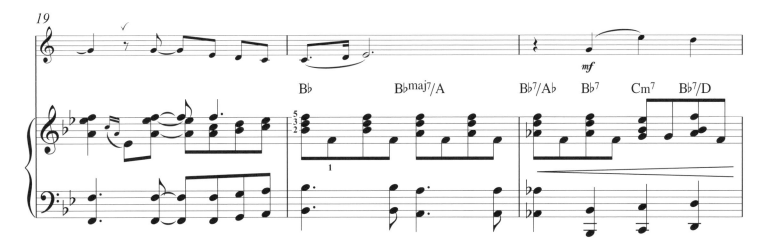

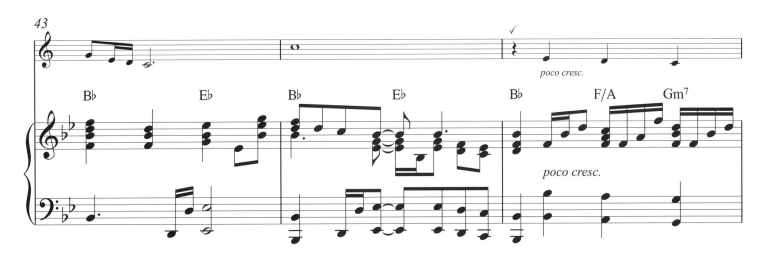

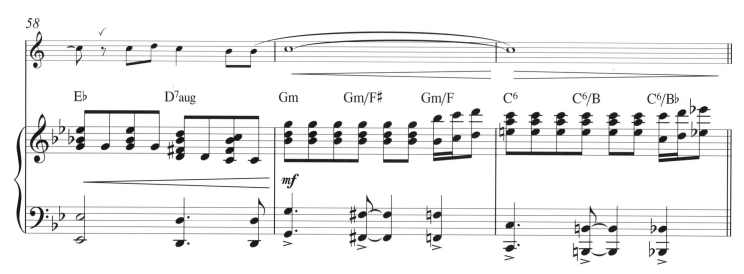

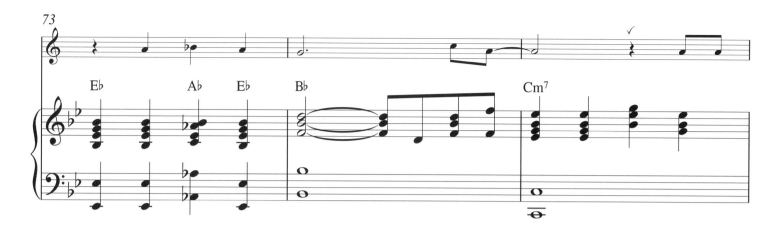

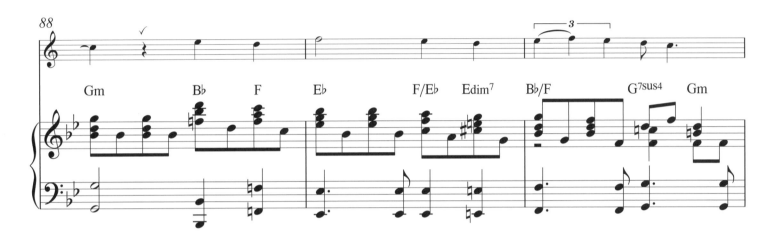

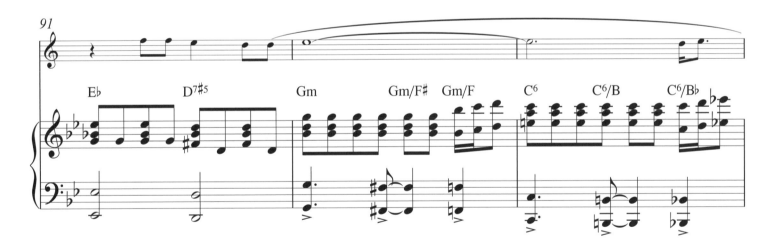

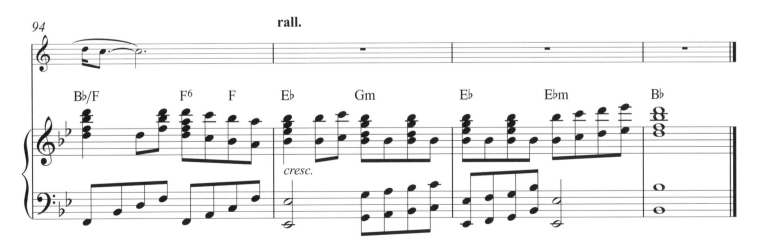

CLOCKS

Words & Music by Guy Berryman, Jonathan Buckland,
William Champion & Christopher Martin

Hints & Tips: Keep the left hand crisp and on the beat and pay attention to keeping a steady pulse. From bar 53 there is a repeated quaver pattern in the right hand played with the 5th finger — make sure the quavers are even as this finger can get tired quite quickly.

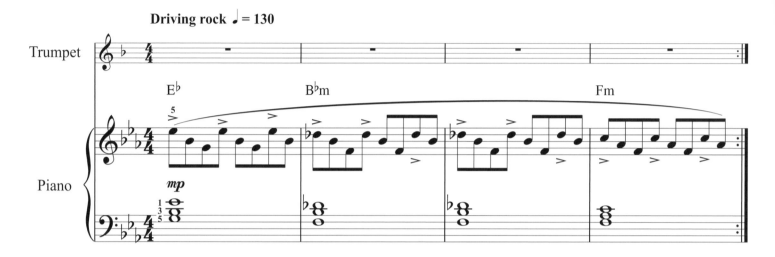

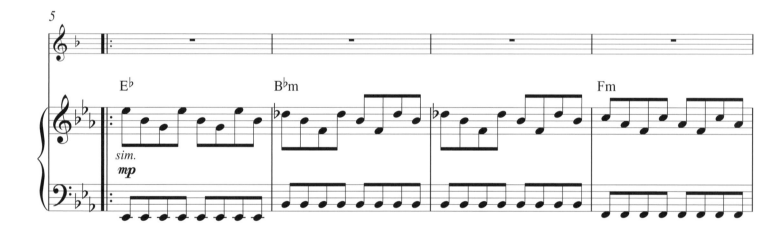

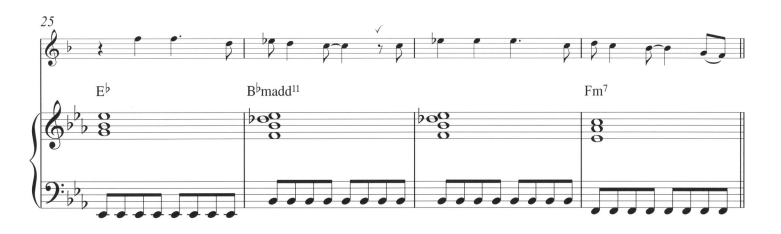

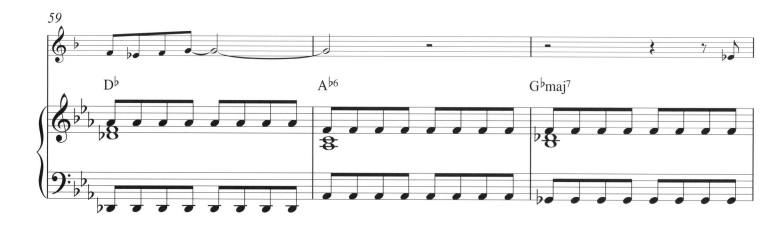

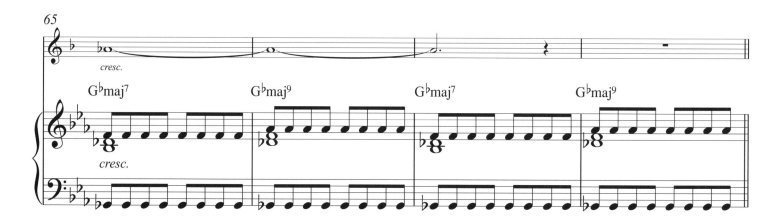

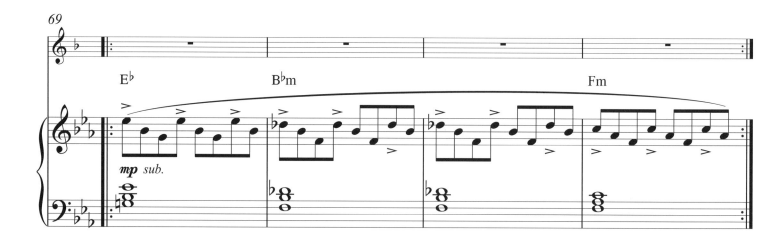

Play 4 times

DON'T STOP BELIEVIN'

Words & Music by Steve Perry, Neal Schon & Jonathan Cain

Hints & Tips: Bring out the famous bass line in the left hand and watch out for the off-beat rhythms — make sure you count carefully to ensure every note falls in the right place. Work with the soloist to ensure you play your shared rhythms exactly together in the chorus (e.g. bars 41 and 42).

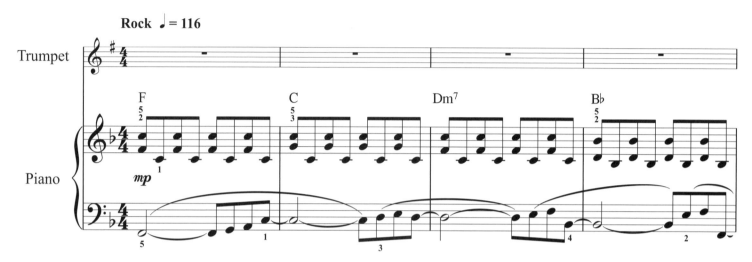

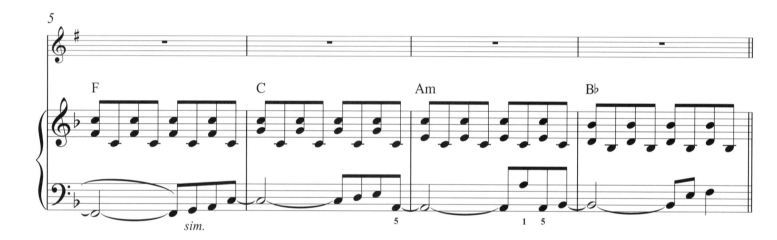

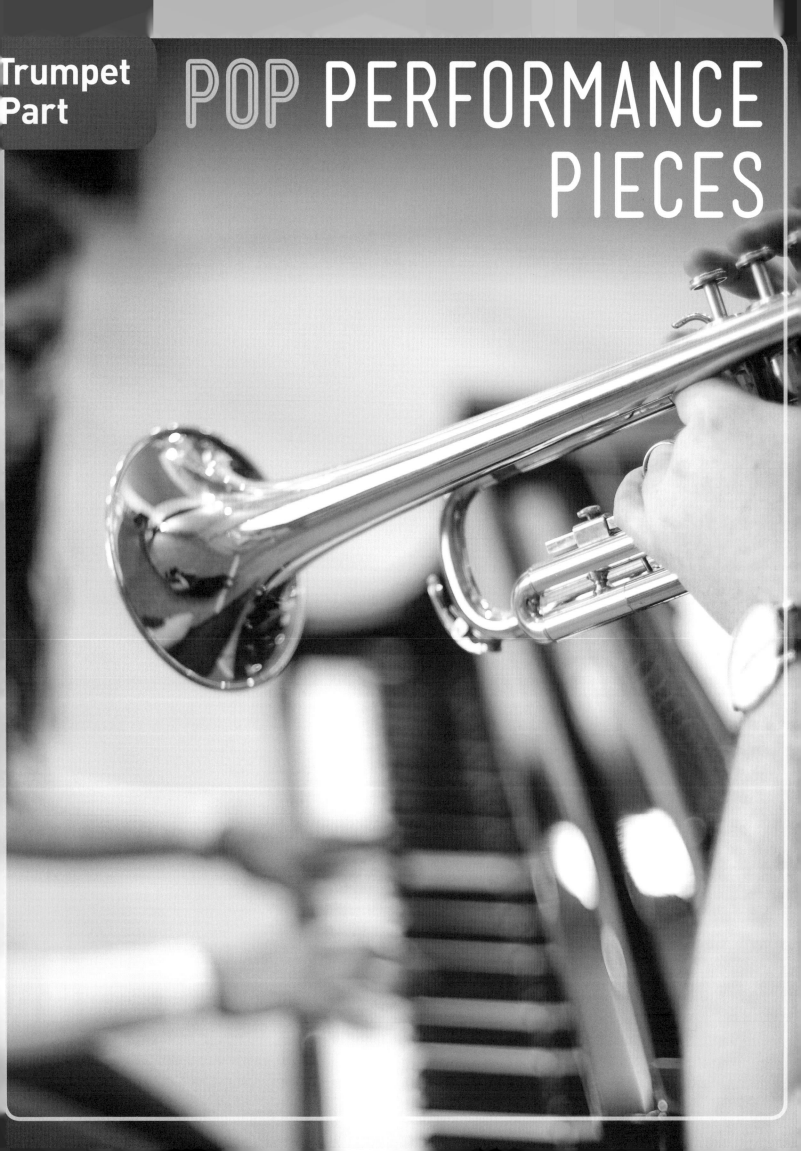

POP PERFORMANCE
PIECES

Published by
Chester Music
part of The Music Sales Group
14-15 Berners Street,
London W1T 3LJ, UK.

Exclusive Distributors:
Music Sales Limited
Distribution Centre, Newmarket Road,
Bury St Edmunds, Suffolk IP33 3YB, UK.
Music Sales Pty Limited
Level 4, Lisgar House,
30-32 Carrington Street,
Sydney, NSW 2000 Australia.

Order No. CH85085
ISBN 978-1-78558-336-0

This book © Copyright 2016 Wise Publications,
a division of Music Sales Limited.

Piano scores are transposed.
Chord symbols at concert pitch.

Trumpet consultant: Toby Street.
Piano consultant: Lisa Cox.
Compiled and edited by Naomi Cook.
Music formatted by Sarah Lofthouse, SEL Music Art Ltd.

Photographs courtesy of Ruth Keating,
assisted by Lisa Cox and James Welland.
Special thanks to the pupils at St Benedict's School, Ealing
and their Director of Music Christopher Eastwood for taking
part in the photo shoot.

Printed in the EU.

Your Guarantee of Quality
As publishers, we strive to produce every book to
the highest commercial standards. This book has
been carefully designed to minimise awkward
page turns and to make playing from it a real
pleasure. Particular care has been given to
specifying acid-free, neutral-sized paper made
from pulps which have not been elemental chlorine
bleached. This pulp is from farmed sustainable
forests and was produced with special regard for
the environment. Throughout, the printing and
binding have been planned to ensure a sturdy,
attractive publication which should give years
of enjoyment.If your copy fails to meet our high
standards, please inform us and we will gladly
replace it.

www.musicsales.com

POP PERFORMANCE PIECES

Trumpet Part

CHESTER MUSIC

part of The Music Sales Group

London / New York / Paris / Sydney / Copenhagen / Berlin / Madrid / Hong Kong / Tokyo

ALL OF ME

Words & Music by John Legend & Tobias Gad

Hints & Tips: There are lots of long phrases in this piece so you will need to take big breaths before your entries. Try and breath in as much air as you can in the rests so that you can support the sound. The middle eight from bar 54 is syncopated, i.e. played on the off-beats. Make sure you stay in time and don't rush!

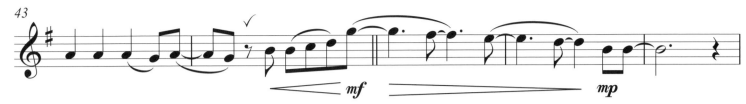

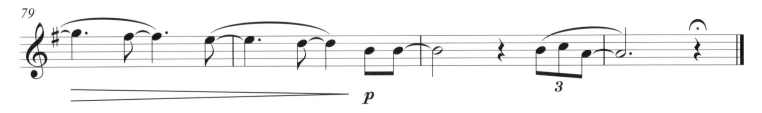

5

BRIDGE OVER TROUBLED WATER

Words & Music by Paul Simon

Hints & Tips: This piece gradually builds to a loud dynamic at the end.
Make sure you start the piece softly so your *forte* at the end is effective.

CLOCKS

Words & Music by Guy Berryman, Jonathan Buckland,
William Champion & Christopher Martin

Hints & Tips: This number can be played with strong rhythmic intensity, giving the crotchets a slight accent. Quavers on beat one could be played staccato to emphasise the syncopation. You may like to have a look at the piano part so that you can understand the cross-rhythms that will be played by the pianist. Note that the quavers in the piano part are grouped 3+3+2 for most of the piece.

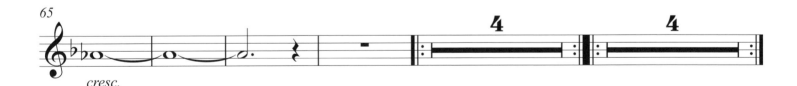

DON'T STOP BELIEVIN'

Words & Music by Steve Perry, Neal Schon & Jonathan Cain

Hints & Tips: Practise your G major scale to prepare for this piece.
Take your time with the phrases and really sing out the final chorus!

FIREWORK

Words & Music by Tor Erik Hermansen, Katy Perry,
Mikkel S. Eriksen, Sandy Wilhelm & Ester Dean

Hints & Tips: This has quite a simple, repetitive melody so it requires you to deliver it in a musical way,
building to bar 13. Practise slurring between F and B♭ to help with bars 13 and 15. You can even incorporate this
into your warm-up by practising lip flexibility exercises.

A THOUSAND MILES

Words & Music by Vanessa Carlton

Hints & Tips: There are some challenging rhythms in this song: practise anything you're unsure of slowly and with a metronome. You can also try singing or clapping the rhythms until you feel confident.

D.S. al Coda

Coda

(2° *f*, ad lib. melody)

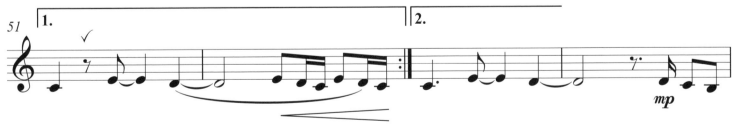

A THOUSAND YEARS

Words & Music by David Hodges & Christina Perri

Hints & Tips: This piece has a 12/8 groove, i.e. there are 4 beats in a bar with each one subdivided into a triplet. This all changes in bar 10, when you have to carefully place a 'two against three'. Try to sing this rhythm to yourself before playing the song.

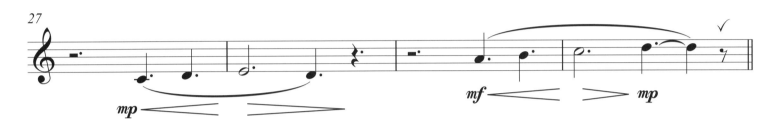

WHEN WE WERE YOUNG

Words & Music by Adele Adkins & Tobias Jesso

Hints & Tips: Make sure you connect the repeated notes at the start of this song. Try and focus on keeping the notes and phrases legato and long. Bars 43 and 44 are great for practising syncopated rhythms.

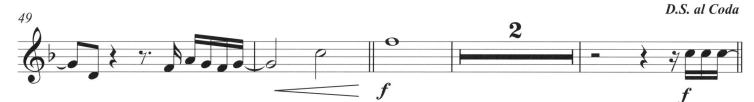

19

YOUR SONG

Words & Music by Elton John & Bernie Taupin

Hints & Tips: It's important to subdivide when playing a piece at this tempo. Make sure that when you are working out rhythms you are counting '1 and 2 and 3 and 4 and'. Try not to separate the repeated notes too much (e.g. bars 3 and 5).

mf *joyfully*

cresc.

mp

cresc.

mp

MAD WORLD

Words & Music by Roland Orzabal

Hints & Tips: This piece is a good test of rhythmic placement: make sure you don't rush the syncopated notes! Practise by clapping through bars 7 and 8. Make the most of the lovely dynamic swells in the chorus (from bar 21).

123456789

Chester Music

part of The Music Sales Group

CH85085

www.musicsales.com

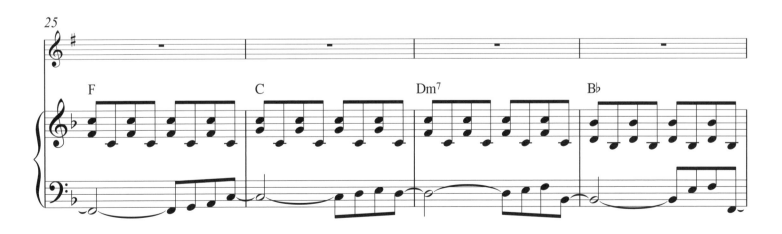

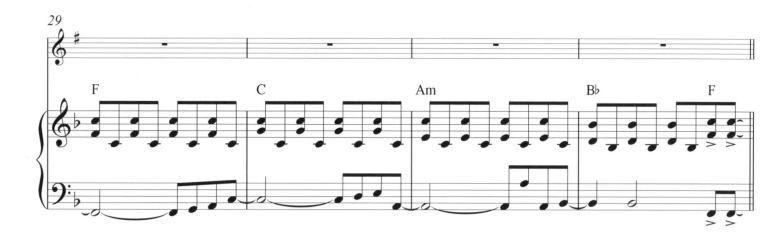

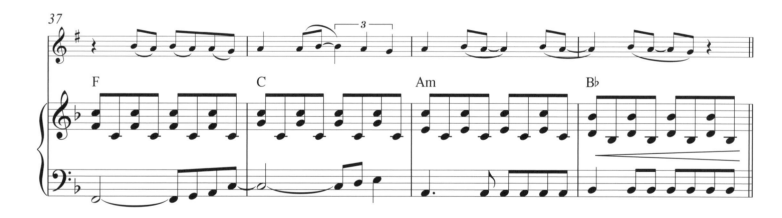

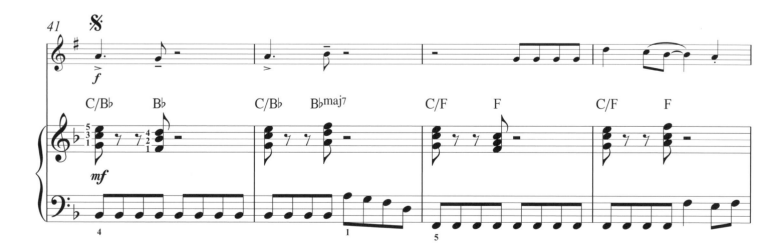

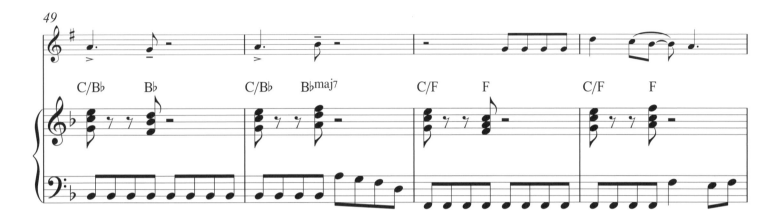

To Coda ⊕

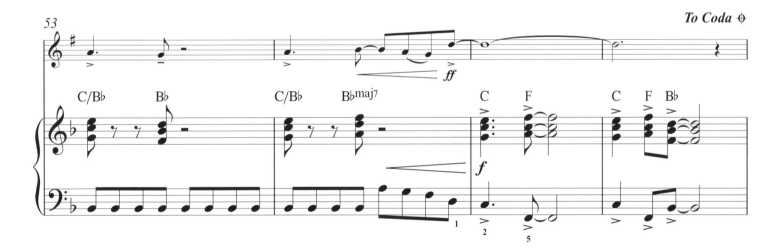

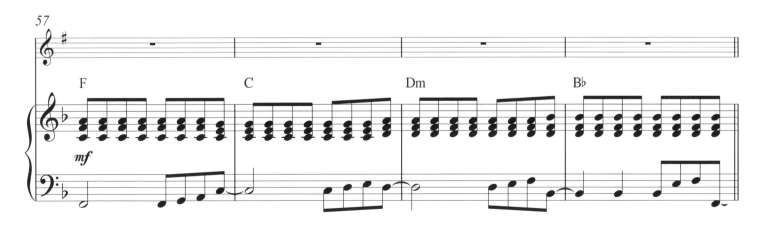

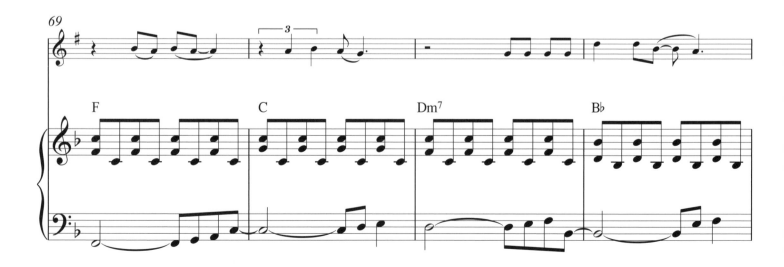

FIREWORK

Words & Music by Tor Erik Hermansen, Katy Perry,
Mikkel S. Eriksen, Sandy Wilhelm & Ester Dean

Hints & Tips: Make sure the driving quaver pattern in crisp and clear throughout.
Bring out the melody in bar 45.

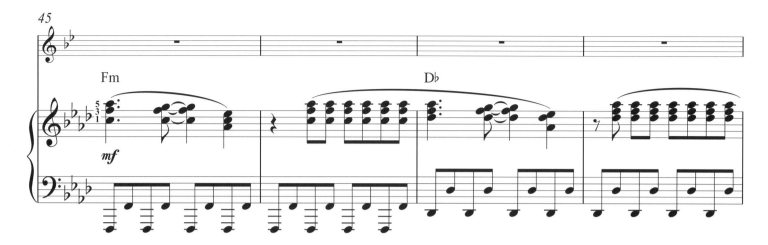

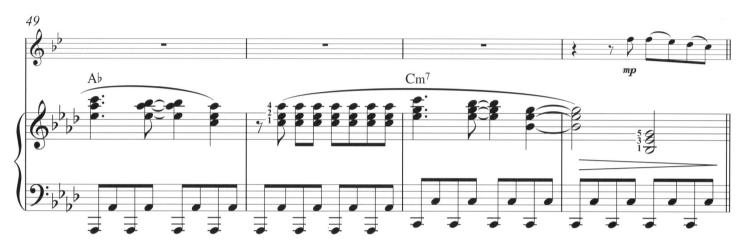

MAD WORLD

Words & Music by Roland Orzabal

Hints & Tips: Make sure the dynamic of the broken chord pattern stays the same when it switches to the right hand in bar 5. Bring out the lovely counter-melody in the right hand at bar 29. The rhythms are less predictable in the right hand from bar 22 – count carefully!

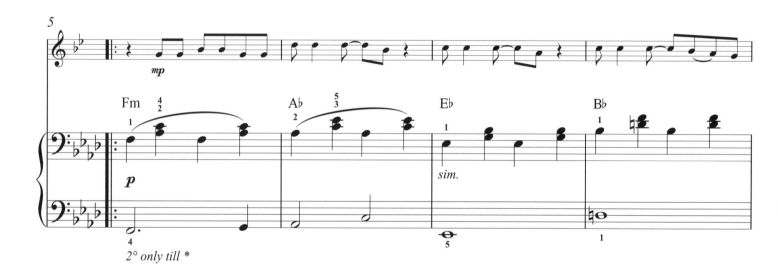

A THOUSAND YEARS

Words & Music by David Hodges & Christina Perri

Hints & Tips: There is a broad range of dynamics in this piece; make sure you make the most of these contrasts.
Practise playing the right hand duplets in bar 11 against the quavers in the left hand until you are secure with
the rhythms. Use the pedal to sustain the block chords in the right hand from bar 23.

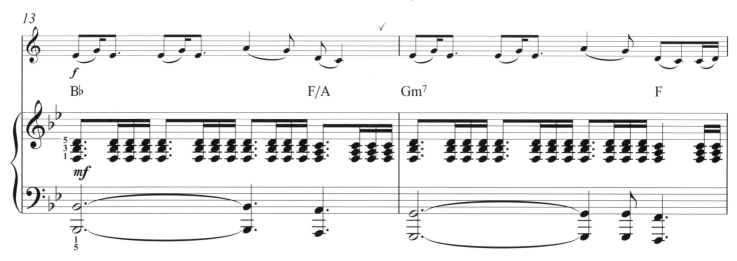

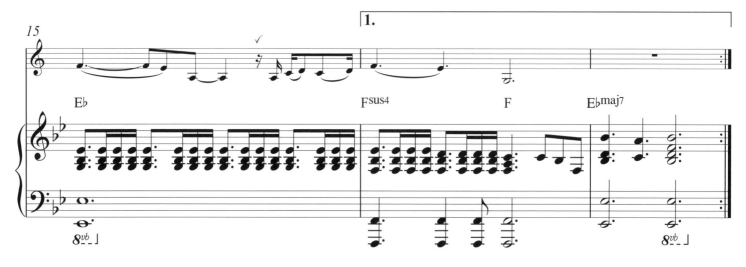

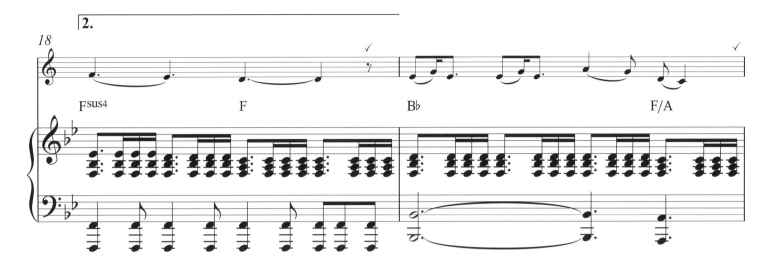

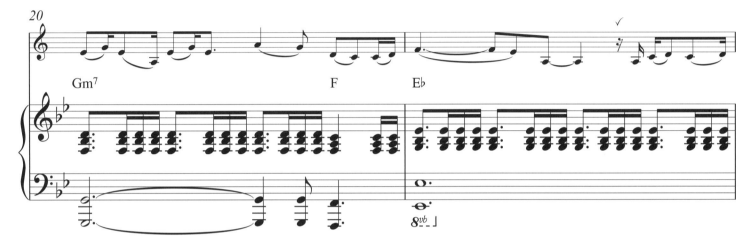

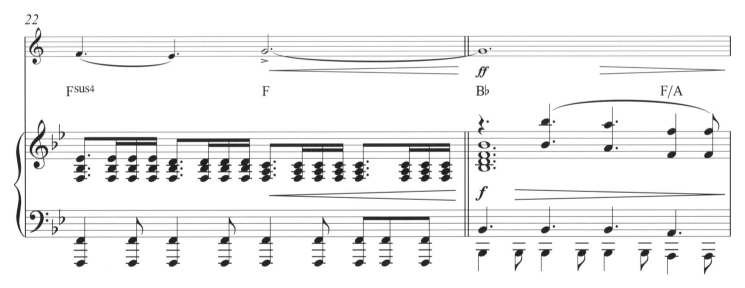

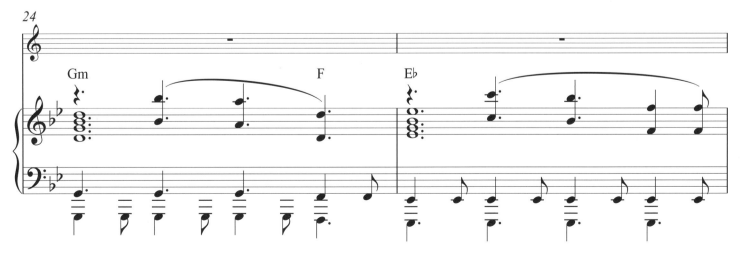

A THOUSAND MILES

Words & Music by Vanessa Carlton

Hints & Tips: This piece features a brilliant piano part! Remember to keep the semiquaver patterns crisp and even. There is a lot of movement in both hands so make sure you're ready for the octave jumps. Practise the call-and-response passages with the soloist (from bars 14 and 40), ensuring you keep to a steady tempo.

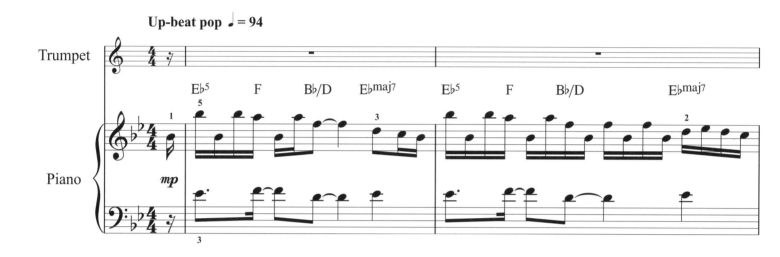

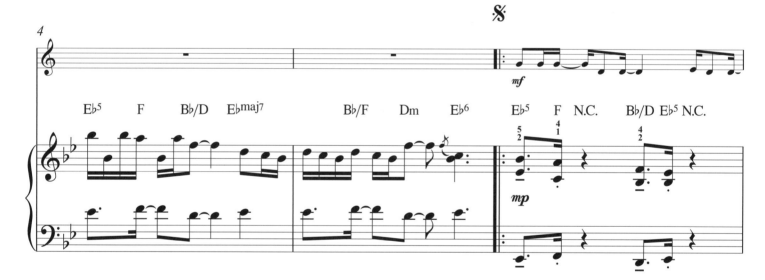

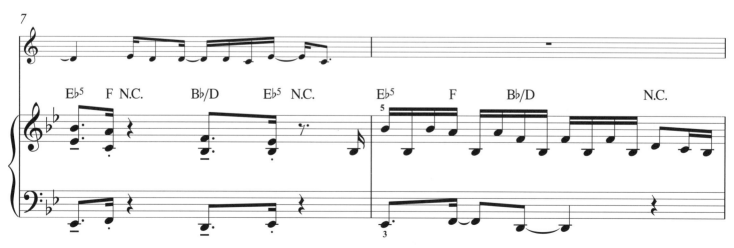

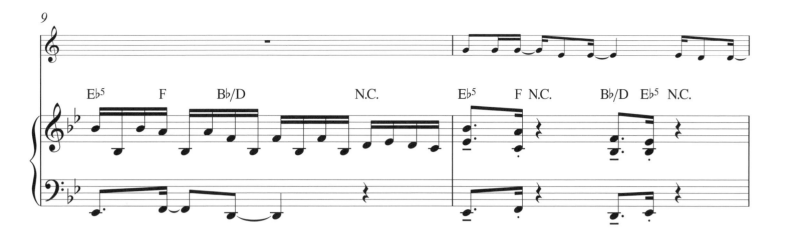

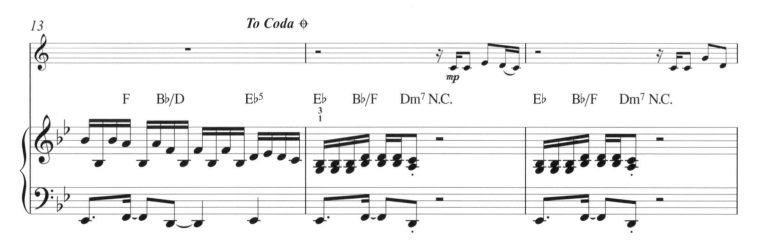

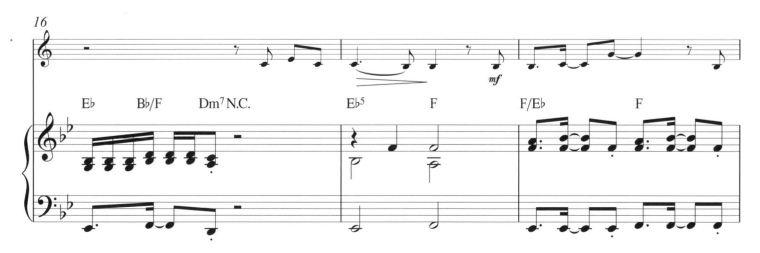

43

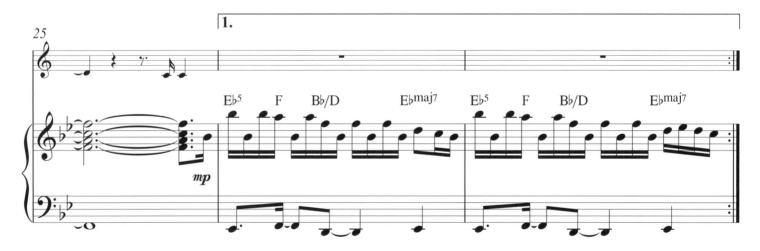

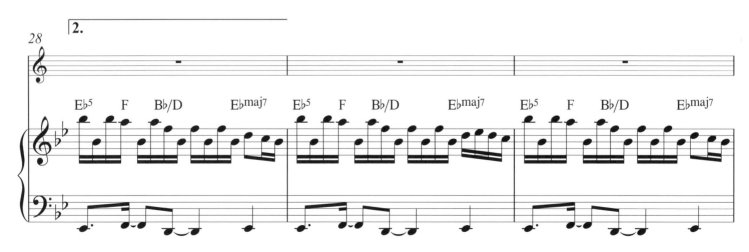

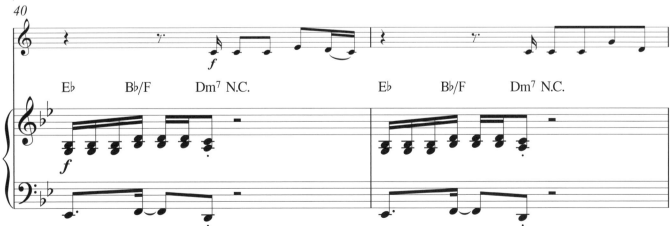

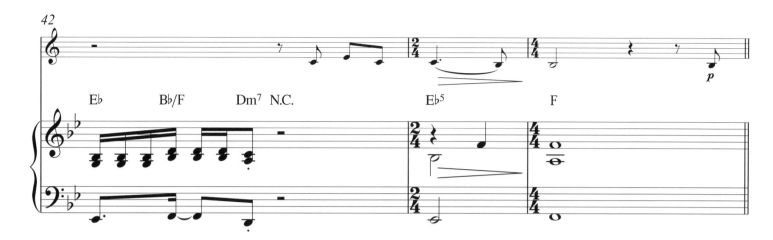

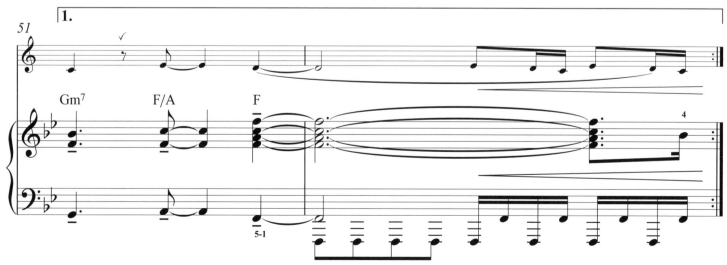

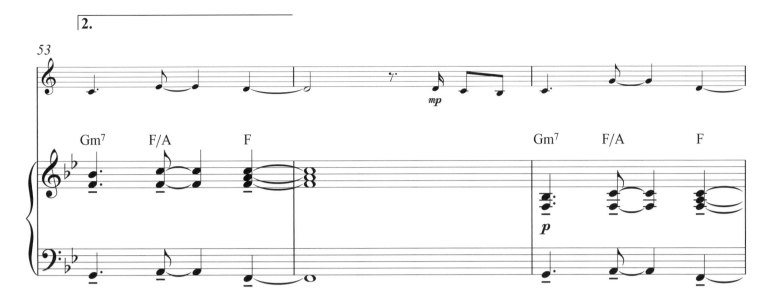

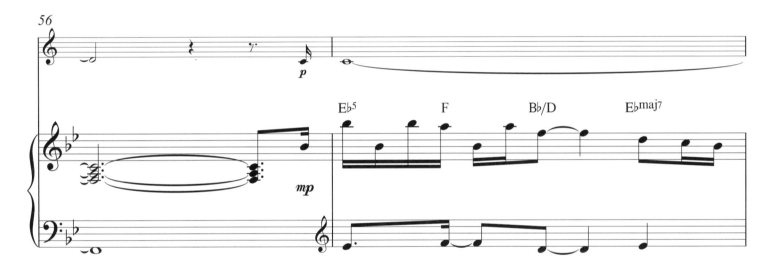

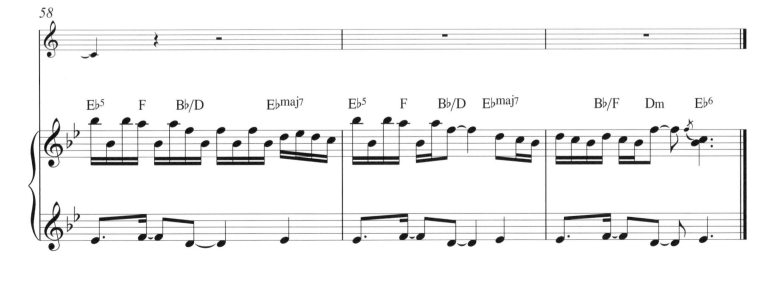

YOUR SONG

Words & Music by Elton John & Bernie Taupin

Hints & Tips: This piano part is quite busy so it's important to be sensitive to the soloist, being careful not to overpower them. Make sure you lift the pedal for every change in harmony so the sound doesn't become muddy. Some of the chords involve big stretches: play all the notes together first to get used to the shapes.

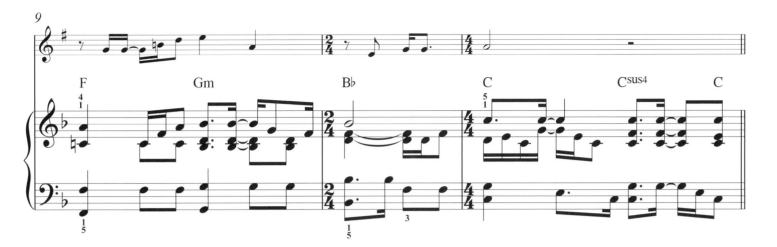

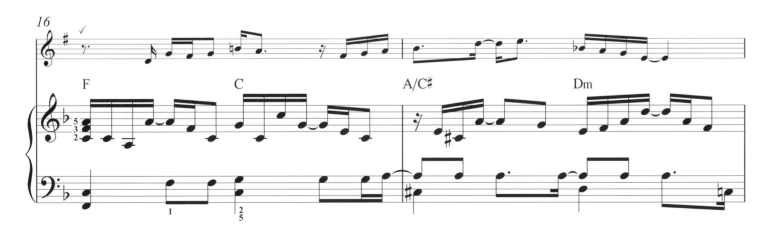

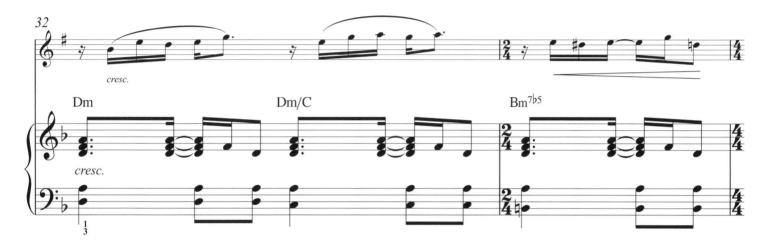

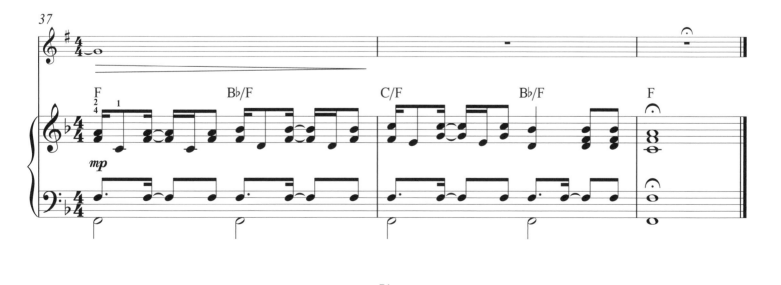

WHEN WE WERE YOUNG

Words & Music by Adele Adkins & Tobias Jesso

Hints & Tips: Work on getting the chord changes as smooth as possible and make sure you feel a steady pulse so you're not tempted to rush the held notes at the start of the piece. If the double octaves in the left hand are too big a stretch, just play the bottom note. Watch out for the big jump in both hands at bar 47!

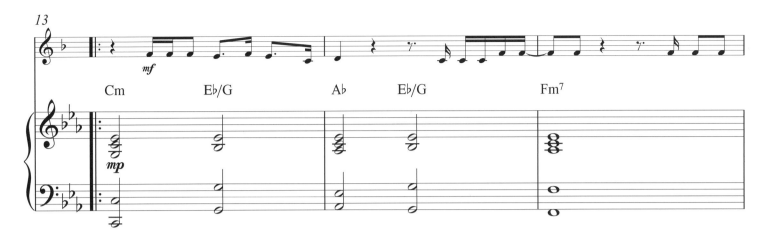

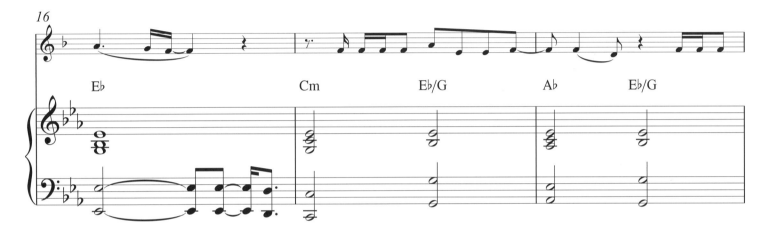

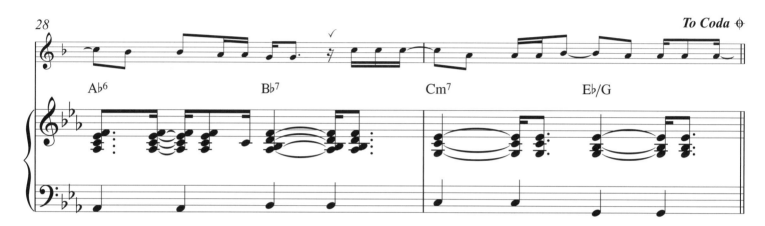

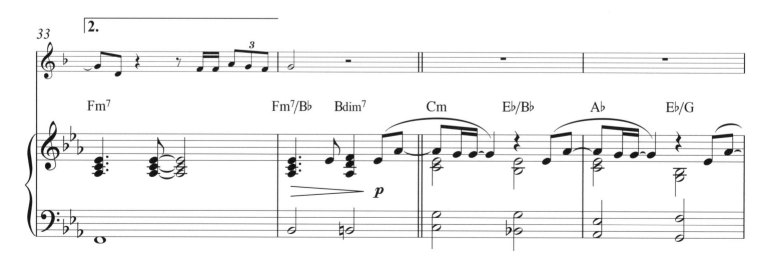

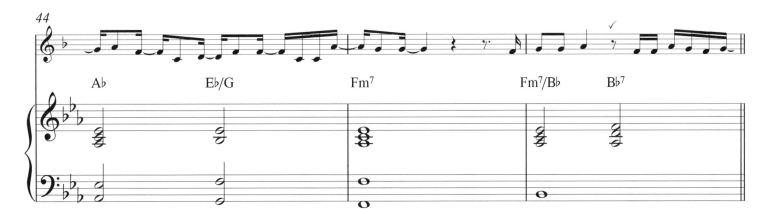

D.S. al Coda

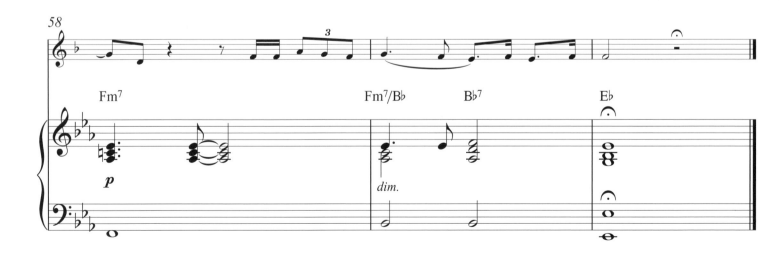

123456789